Autochthonous:
Found in Place

Autochthonous:
Found in Place

Poems by
Dan Pohl

Illustrated by
Jessie Pohl

Woodley Press

Editor Dennis Etzel Jr.

Printed by Lightning Source

Cover Photograph by Dan Pohl
Author Photograph by Becky Pohl

Cover Design by Leah Sewell
lsewell.tumblr.com

Woodley Press
Department of English
Washburn University
Topeka, KS 66621
(785) 670-1445
http://www.washburn.edu/reference/woodley-press/

ISBN: 978-0-9854586-6-9

For readings or illustrative work, contact
Dan Pohl or Jessie Pohl
PO Box 394
Moundridge, KS 67107
pohld@mtelco.net

Acknowledgements

"Keep It Safe" and "Prairie Dogs Have No Time to Pray" are found at <kansaspoets.com>.

"Many Mansions but One for Kansas" won contest #5, *Kansas Houses*, of the Kansas Poet Laureate's Biweekly Contest through April 2009, selected by Poet Laureate Denise Low

"A Hayloft Belongs to Children" won contest #3, *Heat and Light,* during the 2011 April as National Poetry Month, hosted by the Kansas Arts Commission, judged by Poet Laureate of Kansas Caryn Mirriam-Goldberg

"Chicken Egg Grenades" as well as "A Hayloft Belongs to Children" were selected by Poet Laureate of Kansas Caryn Mirriam-Goldberg for publication on the Kansas Arts Commission website at <http://150kansaspoems.wordpress.com>. The two poems were also placed in the anthology *Begin Again: 150 Kansas Poems* edited by Caryn Mirriam-Goldberg , printed by Woodley Press (October 3, 2011).

"Fangs and Water at Kantuhri, 1890" won a finalist award in the 2005 Chistell Publishing Annual Writing Contest.

"From the Beginning" is printed in *To the Stars through Difficulties: A Kansas Renga in 150 Voices* published by Mammoth Publications, 1916 Stratford Rd., Lawrence, KS 66044.

Special Thanks

I would like to thank Lawrence McGurn. Larry has been a wonderful combination of help while editing the text and guiding me through the publishing process. I want to thank him for his suggestions, care, proofreading, and good advice with this project with Woodley Press. As well, I want to thank Dennis Etzel Jr. and Leah Sewell for final editing and book design. They have been a great help with final details.

I have so many wonderful people in the Language, Literature, and Communication Department at Hutchinson Community College in Hutchinson, Kansas, who are friends and colleagues. From this collection of good people, I felt grateful to participate in a writer's group. I wish to thank William Sheldon, Daniel Spees, Natasha Russell, Janet Cook, Don Lind, and Stephen Hind [retired], an inspiration, because they gave such good, productive comments and encouragement.

I want to thank three people who have become strong advisors to my writing over the years because of their enthusiasm to read the works and tell me what they thought: Dr. Paula Luteran, Becky Hageman, and Dan Naccarato, instructors at Hutchinson Community College.

I wish to thank Dr. Ed Berger, President of Hutchinson Community College; Dr. Cindy Hoss, Vice President of Academic Affairs, Trudy Zimmerman, Chair of the Language, Literature, and Communication Department, and Star Gipson, Academic Support Executive Director of the Rimmer Learning Center at HCC for allowing me to operate for thirty years as an English composition instructor, helping students improve their writing.

My daughter Jessie Pohl has been wonderful to illustrate my works, and I have loved the collaboration we have shared with each another. As well, my loving wife Becky has given me a second pair of eyes in reading and placement of poems within the manuscript.

Finally, I also wish to thank David and Meg Gilmore of Leawood, Kansas, for their friendship, fellowship, and ministry to my family and me. They are such wonderful, caring people. I find it an honor to call them my friends.

For Becky
For Sarah
For Jessie

CONTENTS

Born in Place

Found in Place

Read in Place

Friends in Place

Born in Place

Book 11

From the Beginning

The explorers came when stars looked younger,
Wanting better, homesteaders next, tender
Hearts, to this place, an open land, and the
Forgotten from the crowded East, to weave their
Spark into the earth and sky and prairie,
Quickened by fire to remove old grass, and field
Stones, picked out to plow a good life, which too
Soon aged strong men and pioneer women who
Created hearth-cooked food and songs enough to
Encourage the ember into the start of stories,
Read by the light of kerosene lamps in sod houses
On rustic family tables, the place for new births
Across the old plains, with the glow on their
Leavened faces

That became our own.

Keep It Safe

All Ad Astra folk should
Share, of course, what they
Know of sleepy small towns
Hidden in state, cut away from the
Arteries of blacktop highways
And tell about red-dirt streets
That spill into Kansas farmlands,
Un-choked prairies, filled with
Wind moved milkweed
Trilling Meadowlarks, and
Lip numbing Snake Root.

From tractors, we see them
Handicapped, out-of-state
Travelers who stop and stand
And stare into the open plains
As into a crystal ball to divine
The mystic secrets of the place.

For a moment, they attempt
To look for that which we
Have eaten over years
Absorbed by willing skin.

They pressure their pause with little
Time to stay, overnight maybe, and
They feel they must rush to the other
Side, to what they think is a better state,
The next diversion, so they squint hard
For the answer, hard enough to stamp lines
Onto the outside corners of their eyes.

Prairie Dogs Have No Time to Pray

When they notice dangers that come
They dive deep into their Kansas seas
Filled with prehistoric, disconnected
Bones and ancient predator's loosened
Teeth that punctuate their keeping
Among Indian Root, June bug grubs
And Devil's Claw, which also burrow
To invade the space of shattered Flint
And Sand Hill grasses.

They dig to swim there underground
Into bunkers where some live, as we
Will not; shaken, they squeak and leap
Centuries deep when hawk shadows
Fly too near.

Slalom Harvest on County Road 1063

With the light of a slow sunrise
Better to see through the suffering
Heat, combines move like snails

    To eat the wheat and pass it on
    To trailer bins and semi-trucks at
    The edge of the fields; they creep

With an agony to the next section
Their wide, hungry cutter heads
Trespass onto one-third the county

    Road to make cars turn quarterback
    To dodge the hazards with fluid turns
    Like skiers sliding down a snowy hill,

Racing for the gold, as are the
Harvesters, focusing so hard on
The capture and release to rush

    "Me First" to the waiting elevator with
    Busheled kernels of the Red Winter and
    Pocket the weight ticket, good as cash

Many Mansions but One for Kansas

You must take the tour at Saint
Fidelis to become one of the sixteen
Thousand, yearly, transformed by
Devoted architecture of German
Masters, voted by the people one
Of the eight wonders that live here
On the plains to know it is true.

You need to exit at Victoria from I-70,
From its hurried life, its ego, and the
Mischief it causes, to slow down, to
Listen to the guide explain it, once,
Proclaimed by William Jennings Bryan
As the "Cathedral of the Plains" though
No Bishop ever resided there at the
"Largest Church West of the Mississippi."

You have to learn about the biblical
Austrian art, the crafted Italian marble
Altar, the storied windows above it,
Especially on a sunny afternoon that
Will pop the colors to burn memory
Onto the inside of your soul, and
How the eye never is meant to focus
But wander from transit to nave, from
Ceiling to the Stations of the Cross.

Then after, sit, mid-sanctuary, still,
Unmoved, and take the time, because
There is none, and listen to your heart,
To the limestone, to the spirit of the place,
A house big enough to let you know
There is something greater than you.

Agoraphobic in Kansas

Jake sipped his first spring water from the east ditch of the turnpike north of Matfield Green, "Prairie Chicken Capitol of the World." Baptizing his nervous cheek with water from a tapped Artesian well, he watched angled cattle graze on wedges of Flint Hill pastures. Five Emporia State scholars, two baseball players, one abnormal psych major and two dedicated to English, rode horses into the back ranchland and shared a cloud-mottled day. They rode into country where no human would visit for months if not years. That night at the campfire, he offered, in exchange for their hospitality, a report of the barred view from his Bronx bedroom window, under the same stars filtered through city lights, of Seltzner's Bakery that creates living smells of hot wheat bread and about the comforting noise of horns of offensive drivers. These images blended with the acidic odor of garbage stacked five bags high, ramparts along his gutter defended by small Buffalo Soldiers until their mothers call them up stoops and flights of stairs to supper. He painted a canvas too fast for Kansas college kids, about the flowing river of tourists who leave their legacy of gum on top The Empire State Building and why ambulance drivers call the yellow scraped onto their bumpers "cab juice," squeezed from a rich, crowded life. Later, shivering in his zipped black sleeping bag, he looked past his Roman nose, past thick, heavy brows, watching for the smallest moon-lit cloud that he knew would produce Dorothy's tornado to snatch him, a sacrifice far from his enfolding brick and concrete canyons.

A Hayloft Belongs to Children

The mice, given gray color by their God
Slide unseen under scythed summer hay
Loose in the loft, two inches of tan straw
Dross from collected bales stored above

They steal the feed from two draft horses
Below that cool their coats from the middle
Of summer heat after they plowed their
Existence from the world of pre-seeded fields

They hide when children, cousins who cling
To a smooth rope that hangs from an old
Hand-carved block and tackle, tarzan east
Then west onto the mown stacks of fodder

Their constant motion under the ship keel of
Trusses creates tables for tea, stadium seats to
Watch winning teams, and Tibetan mountains
To climb as the light moves to end the day

Chicken Egg Grenades

As a boy, I remember the belt
Two inches wide, brown leather
Folded and snapped to pop
Before the licking

I suppose I deserved the
Lash, a voice of discontent
At the end of a summer's day
The battle bathed the backyard

A German soldier here
A Japanese brigade there
They needed the pin pull
And boom to guard home
And save my mid-state family

The chickens did
Not miss the two
Hundred; they would
Never see the hatch

Slow to Winter

Cooling streams move
Without their flame
     They scythe, they cut
     The present, a history
     Through sleepy pastures
     And rolling hills of cattle
     To their sides, slowly
     Walking like lost children
     Of summer, and feel
     In the heart of it, regret
     For the field flowers
     That must die to live

The brazier of the prairie decides
To turn its rippling face cold to
Change the smell of autumn air
     Its ego frosts across the
     Country, and the march
     Of ice next month will stop
     Its story, mid-sentence
     Mid-chapter, until spring

Found in Place

Autochthonous

Medicine men and sage women
Know they must fight for each day
Using nothing more than their spirit

They walk with familiars who speak
To them through impossible time
Across generations of mind of the
Others before and tribes to come

They feel they must walk east into the sun
Each dawn to make absolutely sure the earth
And every being on it continues to spin

To Begin the Day

I enter the world from my waking
       Sleepy resurrection
       Each dawn
       Washed and
       Out to kill my day

Shimmering ghosts pass with coffee in hand
       They surround me
       To wait at corners
       For permission
       To cross themselves

       I say
"Morning"
       As we pass

A simple congress, a clear, mutual exchange
       Between people, a verbal hug
       If not returned
       A gifted "Hello," and
       Happy vibration

My lips purse the kiss, premeditated and rounded
       Whispered to men
       And asked of women
       Still waking themselves
       Into their day

Satellite Lab

Touching pads to a red-sand county road, Prudence
Focused on the arch of descent, the slow bullet fired
Across the moving ditch and gunned forward without
Tiring and returned, dripping saliva from a tongue
That danced left of her muzzle, surprising married
Doves, embraced, hidden, nesting away from trouble
      Scattered by her innocent pounce

She liked the spinning whistle that I could not hear
And caught its attention with each toss into wheat
Ready for harvest, hissing as her chocolate chest
Broke against the crisp, golden rows to seek and find
The toy in waves, a fallen stick for throw and fetch
And to commune; sown between each soft pitch
      She pranced around me to wait for it

Moonlight Shows Them

Dancing passed the lonely graves, vaporous
Odd partners bound and bounce so near
And touch as breezes moan through stones

They rise on moonlit plains from under mounds
Of dirt, shadowy figures tightly curled, wisps of
Words that kiss eternity's rest by twist and skip

Specters, as fumes, brush their cheeks one to
Another and smile about the secret they now
Understand within the solitude of their dance

Poet Elliott's Advice for the Meditative Understanding of String Theory

Harley told me to go and pick out
A power pole, to place an ear on it
And listen to what it had to say
On a Kansas breeze of a spring day

Being human and afraid, I did not
Ignorant of any trust I had, yet the
Itch of the idea kept a constant push
An annoying nudge, a hounding call

With no one around, I finally did and
Heard the spirit of its dark cello hum
Bowed strum of a long bass wire that
Spoke a low-frequency Hindu "Om"

On Sundays

Before Mass, before Sunday
School, before that, before the
Radar priest untwines the souls
Of broken people and those who
Do pray with their shiny eyes that
Chant to the mother who sings
        To her love

Old Stella sits alone at her kitchen
Table with a cup of coffee, black as
A serpent; the twisting steam rises
        Seductively

She indulges a simple and gnawing
Pleasure with dark chocolate fudge
One inch squares that cannot wait
Though the tasteless Eucharist can
Before she studies her lesson, before
Leaving for communion, before she
Crosses herself, before her morning
        Confession

Bar Car Desire on the Way to New Mexico

Too slow to fly, my infatuation for rail
Clicks away mile after rhythmic mile

I notice the ingredients of her gender
My mind too loud to touch her skin
My married respect and my fear

I see her beauty outlined by a drop
Of scotch that slides from the corner of
Her Spanish mouth, her curve, its line
Hypnotizing to watch its course
Agonizing
To see
It stop
On the
Tip of
Her naked
Chin
Waiting
Ready
To let
Go and
Fall with
A flash
Of
Light
Within

Hidden Membership

Stored until needed, the church's
Folding chairs wait as praying hands
To resurrect in Fellowship Hall from

Time-to-time and listen to God
Knows: the plenty, the sharing of
Group sorrows and individual joys.

They look like their owners after
An age; some have cracked blond
Wooden seats; some open hard

To suggestion; others spring to life
To announce to the world, "Here I am;
Let me shine!" as the little light says.

A few, ill kept, beyond saving, hide
In the boiler room among Christmas
Trimmings that have a yearly purpose.

The chairs become altars on which
Sit temporary judges of the right and
The good. Gray paint layers on their

Hard, heavy metal have sanded off over
The years by human oil and touch and
Rubbing during last suppers, coming

To table, to receptions, to listen to
Lectures, or to vote at business meetings
For questionable underground sprinklers

Pushed by committee. They, like their
Tired parishioners, need some polishing
Because they have become too familiar,

Too close; they remain unaware of new
Beginnings, corroded, in need of revival
To gather in the saved, an odd attitude

For a people who should feel capable
Of recognizing the timing to forgive
And care for objects so well used,

Forgotten symbols for the faith that
Support all sinners and those who
Occasionally backslide, unconditionally.

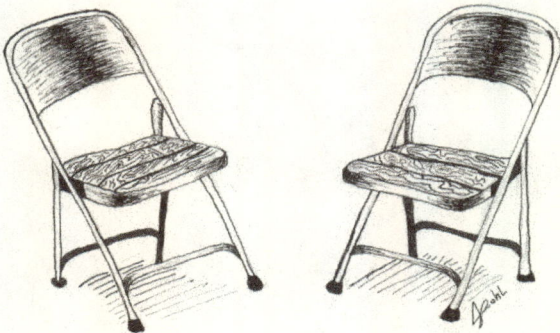

Sweet "Watermelon" Red

He's haul'n home Down one more road
Maybe it's his wife he visits In a shaken memory
Standing at the kitchen sink Glazed with potato skins
From behind. He looks for The mirror, deep with
Cars too close to kiss To evaluate his lined face

Tons of grain, Red Winter Wheat, push him ahead
He stutters up hill, slowing Suffering the long drive
The steep grade, too much To make decent time
From truck stop thoughts Of other wheeled men
Ignoring single hitchhikers Their thumbs frozen up
And of wandering women Who patrol the parking lots
Speaking soft sounds Across the citizen band

Sweet "Watermelon" Red II

His eighteen wheels of   Black teeth roll and chew
Across hot prairie highways Past ten at night
They pick and pitch   Beaches of ancient sand
Forced up from far below   Beneath the Kansas prairie
Scattered upon road ice for   Better grip and some control

The vulnerable back off   Flash followers of his pack
The alpha driver moves on   And they cushion their fear
And escape his spit and snarl By one-quarter mile
The small stones bounce and   Ping, un-popped kernels
Between ditches of Old 81   They fling secretly against
The blank face of traffic   Sacrifices of old Fords and
New Hondas, all prey tagged Unaware and surprised

27

Aside from Mexico Heat

Sad skies hiss pale
Blue and steamy

    Moisés so slowly sips Red
    Russian tea with Jack; her
    Sun-bleached lion's hair
    Rasps like dry weeds move

The cat Felipe
Primps the terrier
Too hot, who takes it
Paying no attention
To her slick ministry

At Snow's End

By the unfiltered look in children's eyes, blinds
In windows made homes blink. Doors exhaled

Their heated breath to make sure no mirage sat
Silent outside. But for a moment, imagination

Along with a wonder saw a glinting diamond lawn,
Farther out, a crystal wilderness: ten new blue-white

Inches for playing hard while focused tongues hung
Through lisping gums. It felt troubling what first to do:

To live as a fox or goose or within kid rules, rocks
Forbidden, for Snowball Tag to become "the one."

Perhaps they would decide to fly at ground level
Backwards to sculpt deep white beds for angels

Or think to create different round people like God.
The morning came alive with no time to dress,

Not fast enough, too slow to carry the heavy concept
Of patience. It was as they always wait for Christmas,

To "get to it," as coat sleeves fought them, last year's
Hats fit snugly, and uncooperative gloves complained.

Driving Through Fog

Holds a moving thought
    Not so much a thick muse
    Though it swirls just outside
    Conscious of its careful mood

My car cuts a watery bouillon
    A broth containing invisible meat
    Unhindered through the smoke
    Of it, the vapor, morphing, twisting

I see ghosts at twenty-five feet at forty
    My radar up, safe enough for phantoms
    Outlined by low beams for driver's eyes
    Behind a firmly grasped steering wheel

Other travelers in time and space
    Introduce themselves, remain
    A magician's moment, then, as ghosts
    Drive silently into another dimension

End of the Snake Moon

The late November moon of First Nations
Turns cold as a Turkish lady whose blood

Cools by brooding, the way the mist from
Clouds would veil her face, a kiss upon it

That hints a brush of breath onto her bright
Coin of a cheek, an offering to say good-bye

To December at solstice when heaven's
Chilly fragrance will nestle over the

Plains and run across the hills with dim light
Illumination enough that resting cattle watch

A gentle pastoral, framed by surrounding
Cottonwoods, which like the deep snows

To come, offer their gossamer seeds
To announce the next season for rebirth

Read in Place

Saying Grace

People brought together
   It's not too hard
Salty butter on cobs
   Quickens the corn
It has to be mashed spuds
   And brown gravy
Nice for me, a dream sauce
   Mama's fried hen
In Beth's delicious grease
   It's all good grease
Waiting wings, meaty legs
   Battered and boiled
Sizzling to crispy brown
   Disappearing
Under hot scalding oil
   Full can of lard
Communally passed 'round
   Licked slick fingers
A drink of holy beer
   Clears the pallet
To enjoy the moment
   With friends, simple

The Rule

When gathered
To a snowy hill,
   The covenant,

With the same
   The adult world
Judgments to

   To the side
To exhaustion
   The bumps made

Up the center
   Smoother glide

Like quicksilver
Children create
   Unspoken, but

Punishments as
   Of their Mothers'
Quickly learn to step

   To climb the slope
To stop the chatter
   By impatient boots

Of the runs, for a softer
   For the common

Good

Sandbox

A small, sandbox child creates his own world
And builds roads like the master, most times
Alone, with patience, careful to choose the
Correct stone boulders and twig trees.

      He knows the place that adults forget and
      Sculpts his focus. His chapped lips hold
      Tight his tongue; there is no need to talk;
      For him, tomorrow is today and forever.

He grades by hand a winding streambed
Toward a dry lake and scoops a cool cave
From his moist medium in which bears
Will hibernate and raise their young.

      His pallet converts the landscape and
      Wants nothing more but his orange truck,
      Missing one front wheel, to drive the back
      Country, stop beside a shaded lake, and
      Rest awhile to watch bears play.

Donation

Without a family,
I shop for gifts, buying into the spirit.
    Seven full mall bags shake my hands
    And hurt my fingers, overburdened by
    Too much Christmas and cranky crowd.

I turn to kick
A blue charity barrel with an inverted funnel top.
    An emaciated brown child on its side looks
    Up to me, watching with large, expectant eyes,
    A lifeless metaphor for millions.

To circulate blood
Back into my fingers and resurrect some feeling,
    I fumble and find twenty-seven cents for
    The unappreciated; for them, does
    The holiday ever come fast enough?

After the quarter,
I release the two pennies as my children.
    From the ramp, they slide with the hollow,
    Modern sound of zinc on plastic, gaining speed
    As they run, each spin another Christmas.

Hypnotized by the roll,
I watch the pair descend through dying rolls,
    Living faster every turn. At the end, gravity

Draws them into the black hole to stack onto
The grave of other change, the pyramid

In the pit, as they slip
From the geometric, tipped plain. I have seen this
        Before. The arcs run differently. Sometimes,
        They wobble; sometimes they tip and fall.

However,
If I am quick,
        I can
        Catch them
        To roll again.

Feeding After Four

What if I tire, shopping the day
At kiosks and boutiques with you,
Down corridors toward the men's
Room, toward the ladies' to wait?

What if I sit here on a blond wooden
Bench and rest your packages
In front of an out-of-place mall
Aquarium, tucked between a theater

And discount shoe store? The tank's
Energy remains charged after
The feeding I missed at four p.m.
Its occupants move quickly as they pan

For leftovers. Behind the thick glass
Slide old, fat catfish, saw-tooth gar,
Well-fed Chinese carp, and a nervous
Ball of silver minnows that swim

Back-and-forth above the gravel
Blanket bottom where, with focus, digs
One hard-shell turtle. Saucer sized,
He troubles to tip heavy stones to look

Beneath to find scarce small treasure,
Stolen by his companion, who

Softly, tenderly, slides behind him
And gently slips her long slender neck
Under his left side near his heart.
She wedges under his jaw and pressures
Against his red-striped nose to snatch
His bit of bread as lovers often do.

Fish Head Totems

To keep up with the heavy
Sun of late June, right
Before wheat harvest

Air conditioners hum and
Buzz sleepily inside each
Car and farm truck

Traveling east with a hurry
On County Road 1063
Just outside civilization

Three miles west of life.
They flash pass cemetery
Stones in line as files

In a drawer, everyone in
Place, and beside the
Blacktop, shimmering in

Heat, a wall of half-grown
Corn that begins to hide
Farm houses, cattle, and

Tractors, a slow magic trick
And background for electric
Poles, smiling into the draw

Going down, coming up
Wrapped in large catfish
Heads on company crucifixes

Nailed in place to the four
Winds, one to each side
Sacrifices and offerings

Placed as high as a twelve
Foot ladder would take
Them toward heaven before

Embellishing the next
Tall canvas, shared with
The county, looking like

Dark-green pulled teeth
With dried feelers and eyes
To become objet d'art

I Believe

It came from starlight
One billion years out
  To brighten the desk
  In Assisi so that Francis
  Could become a saint

He heard a voice within
A depth of blessing said
  A simple prayer, wonder
  Safe within his good room

It fell into deep country
Too, onto the Kenyan
Plains, same thought
Of spirit to a shaman
Brother from the same
Stars to a child of the divine
Light, passing protective
Barriers of men who sleep
Behind long thorn enclosures
With the good message of
  Uzima, be well
  Peace, amanti
  And furaha, joy

Caribbean Quarrel

Deep into Pepys' sleepy diary
    Far from Samuel's rest
    Baking on a tropical shore

Long legged dark water
    Birds catch one
    Trill of a whistle

A tissue issue, Ma Petite
    Left untouched, Ma Chère

Memory, past this diamond sand
    God knows the empty sheath

An after death from small prefix
    Your jungle knife-flash
    Strikes. The curved cry

Of fraternité
    Seeps wet into
    Our brown-bodied beach

Friends in Place

Best in Show

Women always seem, at county fairs,
To show their best once a year and
One to the other, softly feud for it

Together, guns hidden just in reach
In case they have to draw by talking
Through pregnant screen doors, across

Picket fences, to divine the dished
Secrets, a little at a time, coated
With smiles and chatter, disguised

To mimic friendship for the Blue
Ribbon for their legacies, "come hell
Or high water" from spiced-apple pie.

Morning Fog

You should listen to fog; I mean to the part beside
Its droplets in the mist outside within the silence
   Of blurred lines

Painted there among the fuzzy Canadians nibbling
Shy park grasses near the reflective pond
   A time most suitable

For hushed thought, a pensive moment apart from
Angry games your side the dueling street
   The howling world with its thick

Drama, yet a sight like this will shake you, so loudly
Unspoken; it comes from the pause between
   Notes of metered

Music, the quiet that creates the reason for rap,
The art of aria; you can even find it between the
   Hungry thumps of feathered heartbeats

Found

In the country, in the hills, on the prairie
The chosen walk in the middle of gravel
Roads that whisper as a host does to guests
Who listen so hard soft heartbeats can speak

The crunch and grit of top sand sounds
A soft shoe step; they do not need to look
For what they have found, a gift of grace
As they walk through their living landscape

The joy comes in the rhythm of each step
Slow enough to record the seconds of their
Story, stored in mind, of their deliberate
Travel outside unincorporated small towns

Slow Enough

Let me
Live in place,
Carefree, tended
By another, as a rancher
Does cattle on the range of
Prairie pastures, veined with
Sweet waters, sipped collectively
With meadow moms in fields of good
Food that comes from their God, content,
To lie down in tall grass for cushioned, soft
Beds, chewing it over, watching on a hill, jumps
Of new spring calves with small care, a moo or two.

KC Game Day Win: 18 December 2011

Passionate as an AME church, dark, thick music sounds, the colors do not matter, Green Bay to Kansas City red, the Day of Judgment, the ministry pro populo, the clergy takes the field like the Right Honorable McCarthy versus the Reverend Doctor Crennel, ministers who take their bow, religious lightning rods for their flocks, their leadership, icons for the teams that feed on worship from the fans who believe, at a cellular level, the great God and Savior: the NFL--one wins; one loses--all the same for the gate keepers who take the money and give nothing. But it does matter, week-to-week, sacrifice, resurrection, back-and-forth, hand-in-hand, singing "We shall overcome," at the top of gravelly voices, shredded, same ritual of believers whose altar objects click in place: consciousness changing beer, holy and light, the same mind both sides, same temple virgins, so they say, cheerleaders who take sides, whooping up the crazed crowd-the Romans, the stadium; the Troubadours for Christ Choir sings southern gospel tunes, swaying bodies; The bands feud by rhythmic note, heavy drums "Beat them down!" jumping, stomping, pounding their hearts; cavemen and women in pink jerseys scream "Hallelujah!" with a reverent "Thank you, Jesus!" at kick-offs and goals, raising antenna hands to heaven to catch the spirit, receiving it from the quarterbacks who pass it to the receivers, a shared banquet of brotherhood, sisters in fellowship, as destiny and her selection for each game dictates.

Fangs and Water at Kantuhri, 1890

I

From the French mission
At the mouth of the Niger,
For seven days, a paint
Stripped steam ship, beyond
Saving, carried a hooded
Man with his thoughts,
For him the end of civilization.
      The patient river rusted away
      The name, each day the captain
      Double drunk by noon.

II

Under a Baobab tree near his
African village of low, circled mud
Huts, capped with thick, golden Zebra
Grass, which cools them from the
Afternoon, sat the elder Menasha in
      Single council.

He observed, beyond their talk, the
Late herding into thorn bush pens
Of thin goats and dry cattle from
The hungry savannah into which
      They daily trespass.

Then, he remembered, as he turned,
A young man, his face ritually scarred,
His match to a brown Burkina Faso maiden
After his exchange to her father of seven
	Chickens and two pigs.

He knew enough trade language
To properly greet and sip strong tea with
His spit filled traveler, who brought four
Wooden crates of shovels and picks to eat
The earth and visioned the Houet Basin
Irrigated and would plant the belief;
	God willing, it would be done by a
	Chosen people of the inner continent.

III
With difficulty, Menasha understood
Most words spoken and knit together
His guest's attempt to describe Issa,
The darkness or the light waiting for
Them, a people who still ground millet
	For their meals.

With souls exchanged, the willing ones
Anyway, he remembered he too must
Make the half day's walk for water and
	Again pass dangerous teeth.

A gracious host, he liked the man's
Company yet did not correct him with
What mattered most to the sons and
Daughters of the Yoruba old ones:
>Between song, food, dance, and
>Caress, live a good life and be
>Remembered for a measure
>Of hospitality.

IV
Thus, he offered at their next meeting
Before the tribe their covenant and gently
Stirred, with a sparrow's feather, blood from
His best cow into a shared bowl of black
Sorghum beer to create a proper bond
>As kindred should.

From ancestral stories centuries past,
Menasha knew that drinkers of blood
Are close. He gave the gift; then, to see
Clearly, as with all children, he washed
With carried water his friend's clear
>Blue eyes.

Half Naked Banshees

As Kings of Siam, Caribbean pirates, Arabian thieves,
Barefoot, toughened to step on thick, brittle grass,

Fire ants, burr stickers, and stones, they tumbled in
A mid-west village as dark brown, sun-baked weeds

In cutoffs for modesty. Homeless banshees, they roamed
The red-clay sandy streets with perpetual drips off tips

Of tepid noses and found soaking in stock tanks good
Before the open, hot prairie. As catfish tickled them,

They would arise from their baptisms, alternating until past
July between church ball games and have-to family picnics.

Zombieland

The director speaks by row into bright, screen
Faces, which accept his slaughter worthy of *Dante's*
Inferno, another after another, dark dying souls,

An indulgence, a passion, tucked-in cozy, consuming
The inside flicker, wriggling in the dark theater, worm
Like; unaware, the show rots them from within.

Without shame, the audience remains blind to the
Irony, the message turned around in their seats for
Them to consume it, spread on toast with too much

Enthusiasm, straight down, swallowing it, wolfing it
Gleefully, chugging Cherry Coke for half-filled
Bottles of Sauvignon, snacking on yellow buttered

Popcorn, an entrée to the side, as the living dead
Moan for tasty brains if not on Saltine crackers.
Their smacks sound from slick gray lips; their

Tongues lick clean the grease from the film of
Walking, putrid corpses. They kill them with their
Gourmet eyes, gluttons for the carnage of screams,

And, without knowing, they gnaw the salty bone, all
Greedy, one of the seven deadlies, and they never
Ask anybody how many ways a zombie can die.

It's the Little Things

Outdoors, I wait because the moment will come
A state, legend to my map, and a good spot to sit
For a sunny morning read, a local paper, listening
To parting words and gathered hellos between

People, gemstones for my collection, poems, my
Life sculpting content, captured, saved, to fill time
Between, and during, appointments with words
Paper their home, saving sounds of souls and their

Hot, flavored coffees walking passed, spiritual beings
Experiencing a physical existence, unaware of it
Held together, so fragile, with God knows, between
Worlds of atoms that make them real while I watch

The rant and roar of the street, its passions full of folks
Too fast to stop, yet long enough at a sidewalk café for
A cup and slice of Black Forest Chocolate Cherry Cake
With an unexpected, generous topping of whip cream

When God Decides to Breathe

Kansans know cat-howler winds that run
Before storms, the kind that eat half-mile
Sections of man-made power poles like
Giants step on saplings, snapping them
       Laid flat by one motion

Before their conquered fall, they whine and
Whistle their fate, painted with level rains
That razor pings on innocent skin, struggling
Leaning against the push, to rescue the morning's
Laundry on the line as the light of one blue
Bolt, a photo flash, shows wind wagon sheets
Billow a moment before weak pins click
       And release their linen sails

First Fall Read

It was good today to make friends with
Michelangelo's Snowman by Daniel Spees.

A good gift, poetry I can use
To air my blue sheets from an
Open window, a nice diversion.

I found a soft bit of grass outside my building
On which to read, my back against radiant
Red bricks on the southern exposure away
From the touch of a cool September wind.

Laid back, in time, I went to the car wash,
Looked through David's stone eyes, and
Sipped enough beer to feel lightheaded.

Signature

On the second floor of the Métropole Modern Art
Museum beyond the guard struggling against a
Snooze
At the entrance

Paintings hover above the grain of the inlaid parquet
Floor; their collected kingdom fills with
Moving
Eyes, portraits of

Fiction, neo-Jungian symbolism, echoes, hard heels
And covered coughs, catalogued beyond the
Rattle
And hum of

Angry traffic outside, a silent gallery offering credits
From fresh masters who stop those
In frozen
Talk; they reveal

A reserved beauty expressed by "The Red Duchess"
Who quietly commands her low-lit
Room;
Then, slowly, she

Reveals finer detail, breath close, to expose the artist's
Intent by the thread-bare, tattered lace surrounding
Her genteel
Aristocratic throat

Stay Away

I took notice of suspicious activity of squatters on top the decorative grapevine wreath outside, near the backdoor, nesting without permission, created on the first of cool May. A perfect spot for settling parents, altering engineers, alternating builders, robins, they crafted a nest with layer cake care, mud and brown grass straw open to heaven with its exposed content.

Two eggs hatched into gray, hungry mouths, one sibling less developed, one growing to gone by middle May. The parents spoke angrily, bird to man. With each step outside, orange and black wings flapped in my face, accompanied by screaming chirps of dark, deep avian criticism. After the young left home, I took the wreath and found a pleasure ripping the nest from it to maliciously evict its gripe filled, caustic tenants.

Too Soon Gone

On his own, during a mid-May morning
With a flap and fall onto the back deck, out
Of the nest after his flight check, the young
Aviator, a gray ball with small wings landed
      Hard on the world

He then jumped the two steps down into a
Summer's backyard. I watched with morning
      Coffee in hand

I saw him bound for the Black-eyed Susans
Without their young heads, popping up,
Sitting under the birdbath that bathed his
Fellow brothers by baptism for scores of
      Generations

I wondered if the leap came too soon and
Thought, "Why hurry?" Why should he leave
Certain safety and meander with limited
Sight into a dangerous world. It seems
      Instinct can carry a bird just so far

After I prepared for my own leap into
Life, I noticed him again and thought it
Strange to see him wobble and reel in the
Street, a drunken sailor out on first shore
Leave, but not yet dead, and noticed his
      New pen-feathers had paved the way
      For my departure

Horseflies

While exploring
A dusty hayloft
I hear farm flies
Ping the glass
Before winter

Dumb to more
Time, the Indian
Summer will
See its first
Frost soon

The colder air
Slows their flight
Which does not
Matter much

They want to
Escape, desperate
To leave, bruised
On so much
Compound insight

They do not know
To move down to
Livestock in their
Stalls, down and
Out to freedom

For Open Country

The Kansas wind moves
Behind such boiling smoke

The coil of flames fire to ash each year to
Snake through thick, brittle prairie grass

Hungry cattle watch embers fall
And wait for sweet new growth

The charred grounds expose baked stones
And spring comes from consuming sounds

Hand flames pray, another resurrection
As the pop of weed seed fills the heated air

Flicker Away, March 2005

The Pope is old, "Terri Shiavo Must Die" the headlines shout,
And the Teletubbies live under fascism on public television.

Bad news boils all around. Yes, she must. No, she need not.
Again, the hand painted signs wave like flags for the cameras,
And people polarize with the evening's six o'clock news.

They bicker about old blood and communicate by conflict
Because, well, that's what they do. To win or lose souls,
The argument continues: Should we not ask His Holiness
To step down? Do we have a majority vote over this one?

Watching the circus, I ask myself, "Why this unholy gift?"

The Tubbies live with a giggling baby sun with cute, silent
Bunnies, steeped in, surrounded by, a sleepy, perpetual
Summer. So naïve, they do what they are told. The state
Supports their lives, right? —Hypnotic, controlled, mindless.

What nice, warm blankets cover their hard, unmovable beds.

Each day near the end, the hidden gray speaker, their pope,
Pops up at the correct time from under manicured green turf—
What most people want, isn't it?— then announces it's time for
Bye-bye. The Tubbies say, "Bye-bye," then disappear, one-by-one
Like the cursory pet rabbits that hop underground unseen,
Complaining lightly as they leave their perfect, sun-filled world.

—Terri Shiavo died March 31, 2005, after the courts denied her
   water and food from March 18.

Wind Shift

A breeze, first scout, hunts into late
September and slides west for rest.

Rasps of tall tan grasses will soon help
Cool to slow our mother, a living land.

The yellow forests reach their patience past
Deer season; one leaf snaps, one cold breath

Then thousands fall in their moment;
The wave of clicks sounds left to right.

With winter, over the blanket leaves,
Kansas soil sleeps silently for a time.

Lover's Moment

I ride the bus to San Mida
The windows open to thin air
Hot wind blows across the broken radio
    My thick glasses shake in dance
    As thin tires bump along the road

I ride the bus to San Mida
Because I have no other way there
I see dust spin and settle
    On my trousers and good shoes
    Strangers sit too close beside me

I ride the bus to San Mida
And cry that I go without you
Back sixty-years we promised
    When you were young and round
    The beginnings were ours alone

I ride the bus to San Mida
And hold your kite in front of me
    The children wish for one
    Their big eyes drink it in
    They listen to blue paper crinkle

I ride the bus to San Mida
And I am too old to travel long
    And look down on my fingers
    I watched them change wrinkled
    Each day before my sleep

I ride the bus to San Mida
The journey ends before me
    I will run what I can
    Though the wind will need to help
    Raise your wish on Salida's Hill

If Darkness Comes

Another turn, the curve of the year comes around
Again for Einstein's birth; the news rings E=mc^2;
Perhaps the broadcast tides with a black hole,
A collider created being no one wants, a
Circular, empty bucket and singular
Bug eater of holistic stars, of the
Bard's sonnets, and implosive
Famous film dogs to circle
The heavenly drain to
Nothing

.

There Comes a Time

To leave the farm, source of the past
Beyond the front door with a first
Step from the place you slept

You reached a point when you must
Follow your introductory shoes, Trojan
Horses for socks, anonymous to others
Who can soon look at their smart style

You will discover Barcelona, Greek
Ouzo, German Gemuetlichkeit, red
Japanese slippers, small, sunny islands
And collected amigos along the way

When finished, you may decide to sit in
Your bay window, more the tea type then
To watch whales breach in the sound off
The coast of safe Seattle or perhaps lobster
Boats from the cliffs of stormy Maine

Dan Pohl instructs English composition at Hutchinson Community College in Hutchinson, Kansas. He lives in Moundridge, Kansas, and writes poems and prose poems. He judged the 2013 Nelson Poetry Book Contest. People can find his work published in two 2013 anthologies: *Begin Again: 150 Kansas Poems* (Woodley Press) and *To the Stars through Difficulties* (Mammoth Publications), both edited by past Kansas Poet Laureate Caryn Mirriam-Goldberg. A sampling of his poems is found online at <kansaspoets.com>. Currently, he has finalizing his second book of poetry, *Anarchy and Pancakes*.